VEGETARIAN MEXICAN COOKBOOK

70 Easy Recipes for Classic Veggie Dishes from Mexico.

Maki Blanc

© **Copyright 2021 by Maki Blanc - All rights reserved.**

This document is geared towards providing exact and reliable information in regard to the topic and issue covered. The publication is sold with the idea that the publisher is not required to render accounting, officially permitted, or otherwise, qualified services. If advice is necessary, legal or professional, a practiced individual in the profession should be ordered.

From a Declaration of Principles which was accepted and approved equally by a Committee of the American Bar Association and a Committee of Publishers and Associations.

In no way is it legal to reproduce, duplicate, or transmit any part of this document in either electronic means or in printed format. Recording of this publication is strictly prohibited and any storage of this document is not allowed unless with written permission from the publisher. All rights reserved.

The information provided herein is stated to be truthful and consistent, in that any liability, in terms of inattention or otherwise, by any usage or abuse of any policies, processes, or directions contained within is the solitary and utter responsibility of the recipient reader. Under no circumstances will any legal responsibility or blame be held against the publisher for any reparation, damages, or monetary loss due to the information herein, either directly or indirectly.

Respective authors own all copyrights not held by the publisher.

The information herein is offered for informational purposes solely and is universal as so. The presentation of the information is without contract or any type of guarantee assurance.

The trademarks that are used are without any consent, and the publication of the trademark is without permission or backing by the trademark owner. All trademarks and brands within this book are for clarifying purposes only and are owned by the owners themselves, not affiliated with this document.

Contents

INTRODUCTION 8

CHAPTER 1: THE WORLD OF VEGETARIAN MEXICAN BREAKFAST RECIPES 9

1.1 Vegan Mexican Breakfast Scramble Recipe.....................9

1.2 Vegan Mexican Breakfast Casserole Recipe 10

1.3 Vegan Mexican Breakfast Burritos Recipe 12

1.4 Vegan Mexican Breakfast Tacos Recipe...........................13

1.5 Vegan Mexican Tortilla Strips with Eggs Recipe 14

1.6 Vegetarian Mexican Classic Egg and Cheese Scramble Recipe..15

1.7 Vegetarian Mexican Frittata Recipe 16

1.8 Vegan Mexican Quiche Recipe..17

1.9 Vegetarian Mexican Omelet Recipe 19

1.10 Vegetarian Mexican Breakfast Salad Recipe.................20

1.11 Vegetarian Mexican Bean Hash Recipe 21

1.12 Vegetarian Mexican Scrambled Eggs Recipe 22

CHAPTER 2: THE WORLD OF VEGETARIAN MEXICAN LUNCH RECIPES 24

2.1 Vegetarian Mexican Lentil Tacos Recipe.........................24

2.2 Vegetarian Mexican Quinoa Recipe................................25

2.3 Vegetarian Mexican Tortilla Pizza Recipe.......................26

2.4 Vegetarian Mexican Stuffed Peppers with Walnut Cheese Sauce Recipe 27

2.5 Vegetarian Mexican Burrito Recipe 29

2.6 Vegetarian Mexican Tortilla Pan Recipe 30

2.7 Vegetarian Mexican Spinach and Tomato Quesadilla Recipe 31

2.8 Vegetarian Fuego Del Dragon Recipe 32

2.9 Vegetarian Mexican Oven Roasted Cauliflower Rice Recipe 34

2.10 Vegetarian Mexican Pineapple and Cottage Cheese Burrito Recipe 35

2.11 Vegetarian Mexican Quinoa Salad Recipe 36

2.12 Vegetarian Mexican Sweet Potato Burrito Recipe 37

2.13 Vegetarian Mexican Corn Salad Recipe 39

2.14 Vegetarian Mexican Pizza Recipe 40

2.15 Vegetarian Mexican Black Bean and Sweet Potato Quesadillas Recipe 41

CHAPTER 3: THE WORLD OF VEGETARIAN MEXICAN DINNER RECIPES 43

3.1 Vegetarian Mexican Black Beans and Rice Recipe 43

3.2 Vegetarian Mexican Black Bean Lasagna Recipe 44

3.3 Vegetarian Mexican Crispy Potato Tacos Recipe 46

3.4 Vegetarian Mexican Enchilada Casserole Recipe 47

3.5 Vegetarian Mexican Spaghetti with Veracruz Sauce Recipe 48

3.6 Vegetarian Mexican Rice Recipe 49

3.7 Spicy Corn Enchiladas Recipe 51

3.8 Vegetarian Mexican Corn Chili Recipe..52

3.9 Vegetarian Mexican Corn and Potato Casserole Recipe........53

3.10 Vegetarian Mexican Tortilla Soup Recipe.................................55

3.11 Mexican Tomatillo Poblano White Beans Recipe 56

3.12 Vegetarian Mexican Pasta Salad Recipe..................................57

3.13 Vegetarian Mexican Taco Casserole Recipe 58

3.14 Vegetarian Mexican Lentil and Cauliflower Rice Tacos Recipe 59

3.15 Vegetarian Mexican Quinoa Stuffed Peppers Recipe 61

3.16 Vegetarian Mexican Spinach Tortillas Recipe.......................62

3.17 Vegetarian Mexican Black Bean Soup Recipe 63

3.18 Vegetarian Mexican Pulled Jackfruit Tacos Recipe 64

CHAPTER 4: THE WORLD OF VEGETARIAN MEXICAN DESSERT RECIPES 66

4.1 Vegan Mexican Chocolate Cake Recipe 66

4.2 Vegan Mexican Chocolate Pie Recipe..67

4.3 Vegan Dessert Nachos with Coffee Ice Cream Recipe..........68

4.4 Vegan Mexican Apple Pie Taquitos Recipe 69

4.5 Vegan Mexican Chocolate and Avocado Mousse Recipe.......70

4.6 Spiced Mexican Chocolate and Coconut Pie Recipe...............71

4.7 Vegan Mexican Churros Recipe 72

4.8 Vegan Mexican Conchas Recipe 73

4.9 Vegan Champurrado Recipe 74

4.10 Vegan Mexican Flan Recipe 75

4.11 Vegan Mexican Spiced Chocolate and Avocado Pudding Recipe 76

4.12 Mexican Chocolate Doughnuts Recipe 77

4.13 Mexican Carlota de Limon Recipe 78

4.14 Mexican Hot Chocolate Recipe 79

4.15 Vegan Mexican Margarita Fruit Coupe Recipe 80

CHAPTER 5: THE WORLD OF VEGETARIAN MEXICAN SNACK RECIPES 82

5.1 Mexican Carrot Fries Recipe 82

5.2 Black Bean and Corn Salsa Recipe 83

5.3 Traditional Mexican Vegetarian Chilaquiles Rojos Recipe .. 84

5.4 Vegetarian Mexican Empanadas Recipe 85

5.5 Vegetarian Mexican Tortilla with Tangy Guacamole Recipe 86

5.6 Vegetarian Mexican Cauliflower Tacos Recipe 87

5.7 Mexican Apricot and Avocado Salad Recipe 89

5.8 Mexican Sweet Potato Nachos Recipe 89

5.9 Mexican Tofu Tacos with Chili Lime Slaw Recipe 91

5.10 Mexican Potato Skins Recipe 92

CONCLUSION 93

Introduction

If you are simply starting to expand your knowledge about Mexican cooking, always keep in mind that Mexican food is continually developing. The primary ingredients in Mexican food were corn and beans in the beginning, and new ingredients and flavors have gradually been added in the course of the past years to make Mexican food what it is at present.

The local constituents start with corn and beans, which were the dietary staples for centuries. Fish was used as a huge protein source in Mexico since the beginning of time. Colonization brought garlic, wheat, cheddar, onions, chicken, and many different fixings to Mexico. Wide assortments of chilies are utilized in Mexican food to give a spicy flavor to dishes.

Numerous elements of the Mexican eating regimen are vegan-friendly. Avocado, tortilla, corn, rice, and beans as long as they have not been cooked in pork fat. As the prevalence of veganism for moral and ecological reasons developed universally, plant-based options began to show up in Mexico. These plant based options are presently home to various vegetarian eateries and even vegetarian taquerias.

With the help of this amazing book, you will be able to learn how to cook various vegetarian Mexican dishes. The recipe section will include breakfast, lunch, dinner, snacks, and sweet dishes. All these recipes are detailed with easy to follow instructions and detailed ingredients that help you out in cooking by yourself at home. So, start exploring the world of vegetarian Mexican cooking!

Chapter 1: The World of Vegetarian Mexican Breakfast Recipes

Various typical vegetarian Mexican breakfasts incorporate numerous dishes with eggs. Eggs are the most loved breakfast staple in Mexico. Following are the recipes listed below:

1.1 Vegan Mexican Breakfast Scramble Recipe

Preparation Time: 30 minutes
Cooking Time: 10 minutes
Serving: 4

Ingredients:

- Scallions, half cup
- Salt and pepper
- Butter, one ounce
- Jalapenos, one
- Mixed bell peppers, one cup
- Tomato, one
- Eggs, six
- Garlic, one teaspoon
- Corns, one cup
- Pepper jack cheese, one cup
- Chopped cilantro leaves, a quarter cup

Instructions:
1. Heat a pan.
2. Add the butter into the pan.
3. Add the garlic and scallions.
4. Add the bell peppers and corn into the pan.
5. Cook the mixture on medium-high warmth for several seconds or until they begin to take on a changed color.
6. Add in the tomato. Cook until delicate however to some degree crispy.
7. Turn down the heat and pour the beaten eggs and leave to set for a couple of moments.
8. Scramble the egg mixture.
9. Add in the jalapenos and pepper jack cheese.
10. Add some salt and pepper.
11. Garnish it with chopped cilantro leaves.
12. Your dish is ready to be served.

1.2 Vegan Mexican Breakfast Casserole Recipe

Preparation Time: 20 minutes
Cooking Time: 20 minutes
Serving: 4

Ingredients:

- Olive oil, two tablespoon
- Eggs, four
- Mozzarella cheese, one cup
- Milk, half cup
- Corn, one cup
- Chopped tomatoes, one cup
- Mexican spice powder, one teaspoon

- Onion, one cup
- Bell peppers, one cup
- Chopped fresh cilantro, as required
- Smoked paprika, half teaspoon
- Chopped carrots, one cup
- Red Mexican sauce, half cup
- Butternut squash, one cup

Instructions:
1. Take a pan.
2. Add in the oil and onions.
3. Cook the onions until they become soft and fragrant.
4. Add the tomatoes into the pan.
5. Add the spices.
6. Mix the ingredients carefully and cover your pan.
7. Mix the vegetables into the mixture.
8. Cook the vegetables and then switch off the stove.
9. When the vegetables cool, add the eggs and milk into it.
10. Pour the casserole mixture in a baking dish.
11. Sprinkle the shredded mozzarella cheese on top.
12. Bake the casserole for twenty minutes.
13. When done, dish it out.
14. Drizzle the red Mexican sauce and sprinkle the cilantro on top.
15. Your dish is ready to be served.

1.3 Vegan Mexican Breakfast Burritos Recipe

Preparation Time: 10 minutes
Cooking Time: 20 minutes

Serving: 2

Ingredients:

- Olive oil, two tablespoon
- Salt to taste
- Pepper to taste
- Paprika, one tablespoon
- Onion diced, one cup
- Parsley, one tablespoon
- Mixed vegetables, one cup
- Tomatoes, one cup
- Cooked scrambled eggs, four
- Jalapeno slices, as required
- Mexican sauce, one cup
- Avocado slices, as required
- Corn, half cup
- Tortilla sheets, four

Instructions:
1. Add the olive oil into a pan.
2. Heat the oil well.
3. Add the onions.
4. Cook the onions well until they turn soft.
5. Add parsley, paprika and tomatoes.
6. Cook them for five minutes.
7. Add the mixed vegetables and corn.
8. Continue to cook the ingredients for a few minutes.
9. Spread the mixture onto a tortilla sheet.
10. Add the Mexican sauce on top of the vegetables.
11. Add the rest of the ingredients on top and roll it into a burrito.
12. Heat the burrito.

13. You can serve it with extra Mexican sauce on the side.
14. Your dish is ready to be served.

1.4 Vegan Mexican Breakfast Tacos Recipe

Preparation Time: 20 minutes
Cooking Time: 20 minutes
Serving: 2

Ingredients:

- Eggs, four
- Mixed vegetables, one cup
- Tomatoes, two
- Avocado slices, two
- Cilantro, to garnish
- Red onions, one cup
- Taco shells, six
- Garlic powder, two teaspoon
- Vegetable oil, one teaspoon
- Salt, to taste
- Pepper, to taste
- Hot sauce, half cup

Instructions:
1. Take a large bowl and add mixed vegetables into it.
2. Add the garlic powder to it.
3. Add the tomatoes and red onion into it.
4. Mix well until a good mixture is obtained.
5. Add the hot sauce and mix well.
6. Add the salt and pepper as you like.
7. Cook the vegetables mixture for twenty minutes.

8. Add eggs into the mixture and scramble the mixture.
9. Heat the taco shells.
10. Once the eggs and vegetables are cooked add it in the taco shells.
11. Garnish it with avocado slices and chopped cilantro.
12. Your dish is ready to be served.

1.5 Vegan Mexican Tortilla Strips with Eggs Recipe

Preparation Time: 10 minutes
Cooking Time: 20 minutes
Serving: 4

Ingredients:

- Sliced sweet peppers, half cup
- Black beans, one cup
- Oven toasted tortilla strips, as required
- Eggs, four
- Crushed red peppers, two tablespoon
- Vegetable oil, two tablespoon
- Formage blanc, one teaspoon
- Diced cherry tomatoes, one cup
- Sliced zucchini, one cup
- Guajillo Chile Pepper Sauce, half cup
- Fresh chopped cilantro, as required

Instructions:
1. Combine all the ingredients together in a bowl.

2. Pour the mixture into a baking dish coated with the vegetable oil.
3. Add the toasted tortilla strips on top.
4. Bake for twenty minutes in a preheated oven.
5. When cooked, dish out and add chopped cilantro on top.
6. Your dish is ready to be served.

1.6 Vegetarian Mexican Classic Egg and Cheese Scramble Recipe

Preparation Time: 10 minutes
Cooking Time: 10 minutes
Serving: 4

Ingredients:

- Scallions, half cup
- Salt and pepper
- Butter, one ounce
- Jalapenos, one
- Tomato, one
- Eggs, six
- Garlic, one teaspoon
- Pepper jack cheese, one cup
- Mozzarella cheese, one cup
- Chopped cilantro leaves, a quarter cup

Instructions:
1. Heat a pan.
2. Add the butter into the pan.
3. Add the garlic and scallions.
4. Add in the tomato. Cook until delicate however to some degree crispy.

5. Turn down the heat and pour the beaten eggs and leave to set for a couple of seconds.
6. Scramble the egg mixture.
7. Add in the jalapenos, mozzarella cheese and pepper jack cheese.
8. Add some salt and pepper.
9. Garnish it with chopped cilantro leaves.
10. Your dish is ready to be served.

1.7 Vegetarian Mexican Frittata Recipe

Preparation Time: 10 minutes
Cooking Time: 30 minutes
Serving: 2

Ingredients:

- Mozzarella cheese, half cup
- Red onion, half cup
- Red bell pepper, one cup
- Cilantro, half cup
- Salt, to taste
- Black pepper, to taste
- Eggs, two
- Vegetable oil, one tablespoon
- Green pepper, one cup
- Spinach, one cup
- Mushrooms, one cup
- Cheddar cheese, half cup

Instructions:
1. Add all the vegetables into a pan.
2. Cook the vegetable mixture.
3. When cooked, dish it out.

4. Mix the rest of the ingredients in a bowl.
5. Pour the mixture into the baking dish and bake the frittata.
6. Bake the dish for about thirty minutes.
7. Add the chopped cilantro on top.
8. Your dish is ready to be served.

1.8 Vegan Mexican Quiche Recipe

Preparation Time: 30 minutes
Cooking Time: 10 minutes
Serving: 4

Ingredients:

- Butternut squash, one cup
- Olive oil, two tablespoon
- Eggs, two
- Milk, half cup
- Quiche dough, as required
- Corn, one cup
- Chopped tomatoes, one cup
- Cauliflower, one cup
- Chopped cilantro, as required
- Mexican mix spice powder, one teaspoon
- Onion, one cup
- Bell peppers, one cup
- Smoked paprika, half teaspoon
- Chopped carrots, one cup
- Red Mexican sauce, half cup

Instructions:
1. Take a pan.

2. Add in the oil and onions.
3. Cook the onions until they become soft and fragrant.
4. Add the tomatoes into it.
5. Add the spices.
6. When the tomatoes are done, add the vegetables into it.
7. Mix the ingredients carefully and cover your pan.
8. When your vegetables are done, dish them out.
9. When the vegetables cool, add the eggs and milk into it.
10. Lay your dough in a baking dish and pour the quiche mixture on top.
11. Bake your quiche for twenty minutes.
12. When done, dish it out.
13. Drizzle the red Mexican sauce and sprinkle the cilantro on top.
14. Your dish is ready to be served.

1.9 Vegetarian Mexican Omelet Recipe

Preparation Time: 30 minutes
Cooking Time: 10 minutes
Serving: 4

Ingredients:

- Black beans, a quarter cup
- Corn, a quarter cup
- Red crushed pepper, two teaspoon
- Chopped red onions, half cup

- Chopped bell peppers, half cup
- Pepper to taste
- Butter, as required
- Salt to taste
- Baby plum tomatoes, four
- Eggs, four
- Cilantro, half cup

Instructions:
1. Take a large bowl.
2. Add the eggs, tomatoes, spices, bell peppers, onions, beans and corn into the bowl.
3. Put the butter in a pan.
4. Heat the butter.
5. Add the egg mixture on top of the pan and do not mix.
6. Cook for a couple of minutes until the mixture is cooked from the lower side.
7. Flip the omelet.
8. Dish out the omelet and add the chopped cilantro on top.
9. The dish is ready to be served.

1.10 Vegetarian Mexican Breakfast Salad Recipe

Preparation Time: 30 minutes
Cooking Time: 10 minutes
Serving: 4

Ingredients:

- Onions, one
- Chopped garlic, one teaspoon
- Butter, two tablespoon

- Mexican hot sauce, half cup
- Chopped cilantro, half tablespoon
- Sliced mixed bell peppers, two cups
- Tortilla chips, as required
- Eggs, four
- Fresh salsa, half cup
- Avocado slices, one cup
- Salt, to taste
- Black pepper, to taste
- Chopped fresh chives, as required
- Cooked corn, half cup
- Cooked black beans, half cup

Instructions:
1. Take a large pan.
2. Add the butter and let it meltdown.
3. Break the egg one by one and fry the eggs.
4. Dish out the eggs.
5. Toast your tortilla chips in the oven for ten minutes.
6. Take a large bowl.
7. Add all the ingredients except the chips and eggs into the bowl.
8. Mix all the ingredients well.
9. Add the fried eggs and tortilla chips on top of the salad.
10. Your dish is ready to be served.

1.11 Vegetarian Mexican Bean Hash Recipe

Preparation Time: 15 minutes
Cooking Time: 25 minutes
Serving: 4

Ingredients:

- Powdered garlic, half teaspoon
- Black beans, two cup
- Paprika, half teaspoon
- Vegetable oil, two tablespoon
- Mexican spice, half teaspoon
- Onion, one
- Shredded carrots, one cup
- Spinach, two cups
- Dried oregano, half teaspoon
- Powdered ginger, half teaspoon

Instructions:
1. Heat the vegetable oil in a pan.
2. Add the black beans.
3. Once cooked, add in the powdered spices.
4. Add in the spinach and carrots.
5. Add the rest of the ingredients and cook it for five to ten minutes or until the spinach is wilted.
6. Your dish is ready to be served.

1.12 Vegetarian Mexican Scrambled Eggs Recipe

Preparation Time: 30 minutes
Cooking Time: 10 minutes
Serving: 4

Ingredients:

- Red onions, half cup
- Salt and pepper
- Butter, one ounce

- Jalapenos, one
- Mixed bell peppers, one cup
- Tomato, one
- Eggs, six
- Ground cumin, one teaspoon
- Mexican chili powder, one teaspoon
- Chopped cilantro leaves, a quarter cup

Instructions:
1. Heat a pan.
2. Add the butter into the pan.
3. Add the red onions into the pan.
4. Add the bell peppers into the pan.
5. Cook the mixture on medium-high heat for several seconds or until they begin to take on a changed tone.
6. Add in the tomato and spices.
7. Turn down the heat and pour the beaten eggs and leave to set for a couple of minutes.
8. Scramble the egg mixture.
9. Add in the jalapenos.
10. Add some salt and pepper.
11. Garnish it with chopped cilantro leaves.
12. Your dish is ready to be served.

Chapter 2: The World of Vegetarian Mexican Lunch Recipes

When you consider Mexican cooking, it is pretty hard not to consider the choices of meat tacos, carne asada, ham filled enchiladas, carnitas. Yet, tracking down a Mexican vegetarian dish is much simpler than you might suspect. Following are some vegetarian Mexican recipes that are rich in healthy nutrients and you can easily make them with the detailed instructions list in each recipe:

2.1 Vegetarian Mexican Lentil Tacos Recipe

Preparation Time: 20 minutes
Cooking Time: 20 minutes
Serving: 2

Ingredients:

- Fresh salsa, one cup
- Mixed lentils, one cup
- Tomatoes, two
- Avocado slices, two
- Cilantro, to garnish
- Red onions, one cup
- Taco shells, six
- Mexican chili powder, two teaspoon
- Vegetable oil, one teaspoon
- Salt, to taste
- Pepper, to taste
- Hot sauce, half cup
- Cumin powder, one teaspoon

Instructions:
1. Heat a large pan.
2. Add the red onions and vegetable oil into it.
3. Add the chili powder to it.
4. Add the salt and pepper into it.
5. Add the tomatoes into the mixture.
6. Add the hot sauce and lentils into the mixture.
7. Cook the lentils mixture for twenty minutes.
8. Heat the taco shells.
9. Once the lentils are cooked add it in the taco shells.
10. Add the fresh salsa on the taco shells.
11. Garnish it with avocado slices and chopped cilantro.
12. Your dish is ready to be served.

2.2 Vegetarian Mexican Quinoa Recipe

Preparation Time: 10 minutes
Cooking Time: 30 minutes
Serving: 2

Ingredients:

- Minced garlic, two tablespoon
- Red chili pepper, two tablespoon
- Cilantro, half cup
- Chopped coriander, half cup
- Olive oil, two tablespoon
- Chopped tomatoes, one cup
- Quinoa, one cup
- Chili powder, one teaspoon
- Red onion, one cup
- Red Mexican sauce, one cup

- Mexican paprika, half teaspoon
- Water, one cup

Instructions:
1. Take a pan.
2. Add in the oil and red onions.
3. Cook the onions until they become soft and fragrant.
4. Add in the chopped garlic.
5. Cook the mixture and add the tomatoes into it.
6. Add the spices.
7. When the tomatoes are done, add the quinoa into it.
8. Add in the water and sauce.
9. Mix the ingredients carefully and cover the pan.
10. When the quinoa is done, add in the cilantro and coriander.
11. Mix the quinoa and let it cook for an additional five minutes.
12. Your dish is ready to be served.

2.3 Vegetarian Mexican Tortilla Pizza Recipe

Preparation Time: 10 minutes
Cooking Time: 30 minutes
Serving: 4

Ingredients:
- Red chili pepper, two tablespoon
- Butter, half cup
- Tortillas, as required
- Red Mexican sauce, a quarter cup

- Black beans, one cup
- Red onions, half cup
- Corn, half cup
- Tomatoes, one cup
- Butter, for greasing
- Mixed cheese, one cup
- Red bell peppers, one cup

Instructions:
1. Take a large pan.
2. Add the butter, beans and corn into the pan.
3. Add the spices and tomatoes into the pan.
4. Cook the mixture well and then dish it out.
5. Lay the tortilla sheets on a baking tray.
6. Add the bean and corn mixture on top.
7. Add the red onions on top.
8. Add the bell peppers and cheese on top of the beans.
9. Bake the tortillas until the cheese melts.
10. The dish is ready to be served.

2.4 Vegetarian Mexican Stuffed Peppers with Walnut Cheese Sauce Recipe

Preparation Time: 10 minutes
Cooking Time: 20 minutes
Serving: 2

Ingredients:

- Mexican paprika, half teaspoon
- Water, half cup
- Hot sauce, one cup
- Mixed vegetables, two cups

- Minced garlic, two tablespoon
- Corn, half cup
- Powdered cumin, one tablespoon
- Salt, to taste
- Black pepper, to taste
- Cumin powder, one teaspoon
- Red onion, one cup
- Cilantro, half cup
- Olive oil, two tablespoon
- Bell peppers, four
- Chopped tomatoes, one cup
- Walnut cheese sauce, one cup

Instructions:
1. Take a pan.
2. Add oil and onions into it.
3. Cook the onions until they are fragrant.
4. Add the garlic and mix it until its color changes.
5. Add in the chopped tomatoes.
6. Add the vegetables and corn.
7. Add in the spices, salt, and pepper.
8. Add in the water and cover your pan.
9. Cook the mixture for fifteen minutes.
10. Clean the bell peppers from inside.
11. Add the mixture into the bell peppers.
12. Add the walnut cheese sauce on top.
13. Place the bell peppers in a baking tray.
14. Bake the bell peppers for ten minutes.
15. Garnish the cilantro on top.
16. Your dish is ready to be served.

2.5 Vegetarian Mexican Burrito Recipe

Preparation Time: 10 minutes
Cooking Time: 20 minutes
Serving: 2

Ingredients:

- Olive oil, two tablespoon
- Salt to taste
- Pepper to taste
- Paprika, one tablespoon
- Onion diced, one cup
- Parsley, one tablespoon
- Black beans, one cup
- Mixed cheese, one cup
- Tomatoes, one cup
- Jalapeno slices, as required
- Mexican red sauce, one cup
- Avocado slices, as required
- Corn, half cup
- Tortilla sheets, four
- Fresh salsa, one cup

Instructions:
1. Add the olive oil into a pan.
2. Heat the oil well.
3. Add the onions.
4. Cook the onions well until they turn soft.
5. Add parsley, paprika and tomatoes.
6. Cook them for five minutes.
7. Add the black beans and corn.
8. Continue to cook the ingredients for a few minutes.

9. Lay the mixture onto a tortilla sheet.
10. Add the Mexican sauce on top of the beans and corn.
11. Add the rest of the ingredients on top and roll it into a burrito.
12. Heat the burrito to make sure the cheese melts.
13. You can serve it with extra Mexican sauce on the side.
14. Your dish is ready to be served.

2.6 Vegetarian Mexican Tortilla Pan Recipe

Preparation Time: 10 minutes
Cooking Time: 30 minutes
Serving: 4

Ingredients:

- Red chili pepper, two tablespoon
- Butter, half cup
- Tortillas, four
- Red Mexican sauce, a quarter cup
- Mixed vegetables, one cup
- Red onions, half cup
- Corn, half cup
- Tomatoes, one cup
- Butter, for greasing
- Mixed cheese, one cup
- Red bell peppers, one cup

Instructions:
1. Take a large pan.
2. Add the butter, vegetables and corn into the pan.
3. Add the spices and tomatoes into the pan.

4. Cook the mixture well and then dish it out.
5. Lay the tortilla sheets on a baking tray.
6. Add the vegetables and corn mixture on top.
7. Add the red onions on top.
8. Add the bell peppers and cheese on top of the vegetables.
9. Add another tortilla on top and repeat the procedure for all the tortillas.
10. Grill the tortillas until the cheese melts.
11. The dish is ready to be served.

2.7 Vegetarian Mexican Spinach and Tomato Quesadilla Recipe

Preparation Time: 10 minutes
Cooking Time: 20 minutes
Serving: 2

Ingredients:

- Olive oil, two tablespoon
- Garlic powder, one tablespoon
- Salt to taste
- Mexican Pepper to taste
- Paprika, one tablespoon
- Onion diced, one cup
- Parsley, one tablespoon
- Spinach, one cup
- Tomatoes, one cup
- Guacamole paste, one cup
- Pepper jack cheese, two cups
- Tortilla sheets, four

Instructions:

1. Take a pan and add olive oil into it.
2. Heat the oil well.
3. Add parsley, garlic powder, paprika and tomatoes.
4. Cook them for five minutes.
5. Then you can add onions.
6. Add spinach pieces into the pan.
7. Continue to cook the ingredients for few minutes.
8. Lay the mixture onto a tortilla sheet.
9. Add the guacamole mixture on top of the spinach and tomatoes.
10. Add the cheese blend on top and cover it with another tortilla.
11. Cook the tortilla sheets on both sides.
12. You can serve it with any sauce of your choice.
13. Your dish is ready to be served.

2.8 Vegetarian Fuego Del Dragon Recipe

Preparation Time: 30 minutes
Cooking Time: 10 minutes
Serving: 4

Ingredients:

- Olive oil, one teaspoon
- Garlic powder, one tablespoon
- Salt to taste
- Mexican chili sauce, one cup
- Paprika, one tablespoon
- Onion diced, one cup
- Parsley, one tablespoon
- Cooked rice, one cup
- Tomatoes, one cup
- Guacamole paste, one cup

- Pepper jack cheese, two cups
- Chili pickle, one cup
- Fresh salsa, one cup

Instructions:
1. Take a pan.
2. Add in the oil and onions.
3. Cook the onions until they become soft and fragrant.
4. Add the garlic powder into the pan.
5. Cook the mixture and add the tomatoes into it.
6. Add the cooked rice into the mixture.
7. Cook the rice in the mixture and then dish it out.
8. Add the rice in a bowl.
9. Add the cheese, the guacamole paste, the chili sauce and pickles all to the bowl.
10. Garnish the dish with chopped parsley leaves.
11. Your dish is ready to be served.

2.9 Vegetarian Mexican Oven Roasted Cauliflower Rice Recipe

Preparation Time: 10 minutes
Cooking Time: 30 minutes
Serving: 2

Ingredients:

- Minced garlic, two tablespoon
- Red chili pepper, two tablespoon
- Cilantro, half cup
- Chopped coriander, half cup
- Olive oil, two tablespoon
- Chopped tomatoes, one cup
- Cauliflower rice, one cup
- Chili powder, one teaspoon
- Red onion, one cup
- Red Mexican sauce, one cup
- Mexican paprika, half teaspoon
- Water, one cup

Instructions:
1. Take a pan.
2. Add in the oil and red onions.
3. Cook the onions until they become soft and fragrant.
4. Add in the chopped garlic.
5. Cook the mixture and add the tomatoes into it.
6. Add the spices.
7. When the tomatoes are done, add the cauliflower rice into it.
8. Add in the water and sauce.
9. Mix the ingredients carefully and place the pan in the oven.
10. When the rice is done, add in the cilantro and coriander.
11. Your dish is ready to be served.

2.10 Vegetarian Mexican Pineapple and Cottage Cheese Burrito Recipe

Preparation Time: 10 minutes
Cooking Time: 20 minutes
Serving: 2

Ingredients:

- Olive oil, two teaspoon
- Salt to taste
- Pepper to taste
- Paprika, one tablespoon
- Onion diced, one cup
- Parsley, one tablespoon
- Pineapple chunks, one cup
- Cottage cheese, one cup
- Tomatoes, one cup
- Jalapeno slices, as required
- Mexican hot sauce, one cup
- Avocado slices, as required
- Tortilla sheets, four
- Fresh salsa, one cup

Instructions:
1. Add the olive oil into a pan.
2. Heat the oil well.
3. Add the onions.
4. Cook the onions well until they turn soft.
5. Add parsley, paprika and tomatoes.
6. Cook them for five minutes.
7. Add the pineapple chunks into the mixture.
8. Continue to cook the ingredients for a few minutes.

9. Lay the mixture onto a tortilla sheet.
10. Add the hot sauce on top of the pineapple chunks.
11. Add the rest of the ingredients on top and roll it into a burrito.
12. Heat the burrito.
13. Your dish is ready to be served.

2.11 Vegetarian Mexican Quinoa Salad Recipe

Preparation Time: 30 minutes
Cooking Time: 10 minutes
Serving: 4

Ingredients:

- Onions, one
- Chopped garlic, one teaspoon
- Mexican hot sauce, half cup
- Chopped cilantro, half tablespoon
- Cooked quinoa, two cups
- Tortilla chips, as required
- Fresh salsa, half cup
- Avocado slices, one cup
- Salt, to taste
- Black pepper, to taste
- Chopped fresh chives, as required
- Cooked corn, half cup
- Cooked black beans, half cup
- Mexican salad dressing, one cup

Instructions:
1. Take a large bowl.

2. Add all the ingredients into the bowl.
3. Mix all the ingredients well.
4. Add the tortilla chips on top of the salad.
5. Your dish is ready to be served.

2.12 Vegetarian Mexican Sweet Potato Burrito Recipe

Preparation Time: 10 minutes
Cooking Time: 20 minutes
Serving: 2

Ingredients:

- Olive oil, one tablespoon
- Salt to taste
- Pepper to taste
- Paprika, one tablespoon
- Onion diced, one cup
- Parsley, two tablespoon
- Sweet potato chunks, one cup
- Mixed cheese, one cup
- Tomatoes, one cup
- Cumin powder, one tablespoon
- Jalapeno slices, as required
- Mexican chili sauce, one cup
- Avocado slices, as required
- Tortilla sheets, four
- Fresh salsa, one cup

Instructions:
1. Add the olive oil into a pan.
2. Heat the oil well.
3. Add the onions.

4. Cook the onions well until they turn soft.
5. Add cumin powder, paprika and tomatoes.
6. Cook them for five minutes.
7. Add the sweet potato chunks into the mixture.
8. Continue to cook the ingredients for a few minutes.
9. Lay the mixture onto a tortilla sheet.
10. Add the chili sauce on top of the sweet potato.
11. Add the rest of the ingredients on top and roll it into a burrito.
12. Heat the burrito so that the cheese melts.
13. Your dish is ready to be served.

2.13 Vegetarian Mexican Corn Salad Recipe

Preparation Time: 30 minutes
Cooking Time: 10 minutes
Serving: 4

Ingredients:

- Onions, one
- Chopped garlic, one teaspoon
- Mexican hot sauce, half cup
- Chopped cilantro, half tablespoon
- Boiled corn, two cups
- Tortilla chips, as required
- Fresh salsa, half cup

- Avocado slices, one cup
- Salt, to taste
- Black pepper, to taste
- Chopped fresh chives, as required
- Mexican salad dressing, one cup

Instructions:
1. Take a large bowl.
2. Add all the ingredients into the bowl.
3. Mix all the ingredients well.
4. Add the tortilla chips on top of the salad.
5. Your dish is ready to be served.

2.14 Vegetarian Mexican Pizza Recipe

Preparation Time: 10 minutes
Cooking Time: 30 minutes
Serving: 4

Ingredients:

- Red chili pepper, two tablespoon
- Butter, half cup
- Pizza dough, one pack
- Red Mexican sauce, a quarter cup
- Black beans, one cup
- Red onions, half cup
- Corn, half cup
- Tomatoes, one cup
- Butter, for greasing

- Mixed cheese, one cup
- Red bell peppers, one cup

Instructions:
1. Take a large pan.
2. Add the butter, beans and corn into the pan.
3. Add the spices and tomatoes into the pan.
4. Cook the mixture well and then dish it out.
5. Lay the pizza dough on a baking tray.
6. Add the bean and corn mixture on top.
7. Add the red onions on top.
8. Add the bell peppers and cheese on top of the beans.
9. Bake the dough until the cheese melts and the dough attains a golden brown color.
10. The dish is ready to be served.

2.15 Vegetarian Mexican Black Bean and Sweet Potato Quesadillas Recipe

Preparation Time: 10 minutes
Cooking Time: 20 minutes
Serving: 2

Ingredients:

- Olive oil, two tablespoon
- Cumin powder, one tablespoon
- Salt to taste
- Mexican Pepper to taste
- Paprika, one tablespoon
- Onion diced, one cup
- Parsley, one tablespoon
- Black beans, one cup

- Tomatoes, one cup
- Guacamole paste, one cup
- Sweet potatoes, one cup
- Pepper jack cheese, two cups
- Tortilla sheets, four

Instructions:
1. Take a pan and add olive oil into it.
2. Heat the oil well.
3. Add parsley, cumin powder, paprika and tomatoes.
4. Cook them for five minutes.
5. Then you can add onions.
6. Add black beans and sweet potatoes into the pan.
7. Continue to cook the ingredients for few minutes.
8. Lay the mixture onto a tortilla sheet.
9. Add the guacamole mixture on top of the beans and potatoes.
10. Add a cheese blend on top and cover it with another tortilla.
11. Cook the tortilla sheets on both sides.
12. You can serve it with any sauce of your choice.
13. Your dish is ready to be served.

Chapter 3: The World of Vegetarian Mexican Dinner Recipes

Tacos, nachos, enchiladas, tostadas and more can without much of a stretch be made vegan by utilizing lentils, refried beans, and even jackfruit as a substitute for meat. Following are some Mexican vegetarian dinner recipes that are rich in healthy nutrients and you can easily make them with the detailed instructions list in each recipe:

3.1 Vegetarian Mexican Black Beans and Rice Recipe

Preparation Time: 10 minutes
Cooking Time: 30 minutes
Serving: 2

Ingredients:

- Minced garlic, two tablespoon
- Red chili pepper, two tablespoon
- Cilantro, half cup
- Chopped coriander, half cup
- Olive oil, two tablespoon
- Chopped tomatoes, one cup
- Black beans, one cup
- Cooked rice, two cups
- Chili powder, one teaspoon
- Red onion, one cup
- Red Mexican sauce, one cup
- Mexican paprika, half teaspoon
- Water, one cup

Instructions:
1. Take a pan.
2. Add in the oil and red onions.
3. Cook the onions until they become soft and fragrant.
4. Add in the chopped garlic.
5. Cook the mixture and add the tomatoes into it.
6. Add the spices.
7. When the tomatoes are done, add the black beans into it.
8. Add in the water and sauce.
9. Mix the ingredients carefully and cover the pan.
10. When the beans are done, add in the cooked rice, cilantro and coriander.
11. Mix the ingredients and let it cook for an additional five minutes.
12. Your dish is ready to be served.

3.2 Vegetarian Mexican Black Bean Lasagna Recipe

Preparation Time: 10 minutes
Cooking Time: 30 minutes
Serving: 4

Ingredients:

- Red chili pepper, two tablespoon
- Butter, half cup
- Lasagna sheets, one pack
- Red Mexican sauce, a quarter cup
- Black beans, one cup
- Red onions, half cup

- Cilantro, half cup
- Tomatoes, one cup
- Butter, for greasing
- Green olives, one cup
- Mixed cheese, one cup
- Red bell peppers, one cup

Instructions:
1. Take a large pan.
2. Add the butter and red onions into the pan.
3. Add the spices, black beans and tomatoes into the pan.
4. Cook the mixture well and then dish it out.
5. Boil the lasagna sheets following the instructions on the pack.
6. Lay the lasagna sheets in a baking dish.
7. Add the bean mixture on top.
8. Add the green olives on top.
9. Add the bell peppers and cheese on top of the vegetables.
10. Add another lasagna sheet on top and repeat the procedure for all the sheets.
11. Bake the lasagna until the cheese melts.
12. The dish is ready to be served.

3.3 Vegetarian Mexican Crispy Potato Tacos Recipe

Preparation Time: 20 minutes

Cooking Time: 20 minutes
Serving: 2

Ingredients:

- Fresh salsa, one cup
- Shredded potatoes, one cup
- Tomatoes, two
- Avocado slices, two
- Cilantro, to garnish
- Red onions, one cup
- Taco shells, six
- Mexican chili powder, two teaspoon
- Vegetable oil, one teaspoon
- Salt, to taste
- Pepper, to taste
- Hot sauce, half cup
- Cumin powder, one teaspoon

Instructions:
1. Heat a large pan.
2. Add the red onions and vegetable oil into it.
3. Add the chili powder to it.
4. Add the salt and pepper into it.
5. Add the tomatoes into the mixture.
6. Add the hot sauce and shredded potatoes into the mixture.
7. Cook the shredded potato mixture for twenty minutes.
8. Heat the taco shells.
9. Once the lentils are cooked, add them in the taco shells.
10. Add the fresh salsa on the taco shells.

11. Garnish it with avocado slices and chopped cilantro.
12. Your dish is ready to be served.

3.4 Vegetarian Mexican Enchilada Casserole Recipe

Preparation Time: 10 minutes
Cooking Time: 30 minutes
Serving: 4

Ingredients:

- Red chili pepper, two tablespoon
- Butter, half cup
- Tortillas, four
- Red Mexican sauce, a quarter cup
- Mixed vegetables, one cup
- Red onions, half cup
- Milk, half cup
- Corn, half cup
- Tomatoes, one cup
- Butter, for greasing
- Mixed cheese, one cup
- Red bell peppers, one cup
- Enchilada sauce, one cup

Instructions:
1. Take a large pan.
2. Add the butter, vegetables and corn into the pan.
3. Add the spices and tomatoes into the pan.
4. Cook the mixture well and then dish it out.
5. Add the formed mixture on top of the tortilla sheets and roll the sheets.

6. Add the rolls in a baking dish.
7. Mix the milk and enchilada sauce in a bowl.
8. Pour the sauce on top of the rolls.
9. Add the cheese blend on top.
10. Bake the mixture until the cheese turns golden brown.
11. The dish is ready to be served.

3.5 Vegetarian Mexican Spaghetti with Veracruz Sauce Recipe

Preparation Time: 30 minutes
Cooking Time: 20 minutes
Serving: 4

Ingredients:

- Red chili pepper, two tablespoon
- Cilantro, half cup
- Veracruz sauce, one cup
- Olive oil, two tablespoon
- Chopped cherry tomatoes, one cup
- Corn, one cup
- Vegetable broth, one cup
- Mixed vegetables, two cups
- Turmeric powder, one teaspoon
- Onion, one cup
- Spaghetti, one pack
- Smoked paprika, half teaspoon
- Water, one cup
- Minced garlic, two tablespoon

Instructions:

1. Take a pan.
2. Add in the oil and onions.
3. Cook the onions until they become soft and fragrant.
4. Add in the chopped garlic and ginger.
5. Cook the mixture and add the tomatoes into it.
6. Add the spices.
7. When the tomatoes are done, add the mixed vegetables and rest of the ingredients into it.
8. Boil the spaghetti and drain them.
9. Add the cooked spaghetti into the mixture above.
10. Pour the Veracruz sauce into the pan.
11. Mix all the ingredients well.
12. Add chopped cilantro on top.
13. Your dish is ready to be served.

3.6 Vegetarian Mexican Rice Recipe

Preparation Time: 10 minutes
Cooking Time: 30 minutes
Serving: 2

Ingredients:

- Minced garlic, two tablespoon
- Red chili pepper, two tablespoon
- Cilantro, half cup
- Chopped coriander, half cup
- Olive oil, two tablespoon
- Chopped tomatoes, one cup
- Rice, one cup
- Chili powder, one teaspoon
- Red onion, one cup
- Red hot sauce, one cup

- Mexican paprika, half teaspoon
- Water, one cup

Instructions:
1. Take a pan.
2. Add in the oil and red onions.
3. Cook the onions until they become soft and fragrant.
4. Add in the chopped garlic.
5. Cook the mixture and add the tomatoes into it.
6. Add the spices.
7. When the tomatoes are done, add the rice into it.
8. Add in the water and sauce.
9. Mix the ingredients carefully and cover the pan.
10. When the rice is done, add in the cilantro and coriander.
11. Your dish is ready to be served.

3.7 Spicy Corn Enchiladas Recipe

Preparation Time: 10 minutes
Cooking Time: 30 minutes
Serving: 4

Ingredients:

- Red chili pepper, two tablespoon
- Butter, half cup

- Corn tortillas, four
- Red Mexican sauce, a quarter cup
- Cooked corn, one cup
- Red onions, half cup
- Tomatoes, one cup
- Mexican chilies, a quart cup
- Butter, for greasing
- Mixed cheese, two cup
- Red bell peppers, one cup
- Enchilada sauce, one cup

Instructions:
1. Take a large pan.
2. Add the butter and corn into the pan.
3. Add the spices and tomatoes into the pan.
4. Cook the mixture well and then dish it out.
5. Add the formed mixture on top of the tortilla sheets.
6. Add the chilies, red onion, a spoon of the enchilada sauce and a little cheese on top of the mixture.
7. Roll the tortilla sheets.
8. Add the rolls in a baking dish.
9. Add the cheese blend on top.
10. Bake the mixture until the cheese turns golden brown.
11. The dish is ready to be served.

3.8 Vegetarian Mexican Corn Chili Recipe

Preparation Time: 10 minutes
Cooking Time: 30 minutes
Serving: 2

Ingredients:

- Minced garlic, two tablespoon
- Red chili pepper, two tablespoon
- Cilantro, half cup
- Chopped coriander, half cup
- Olive oil, two tablespoon
- Chopped tomatoes, one cup
- Corn, one cup
- Jalapeno, two
- Chili powder, one teaspoon
- Red onion, one cup
- Red bell peppers, two
- Oregano, one teaspoon
- Sour cream, one cup
- Avocados, as required
- Mexican paprika, half teaspoon
- Water, one cup

Instructions:
1. Take a pan.
2. Add in the oil and red onions.
3. Cook the onions until they become soft and fragrant.
4. Add in the chopped garlic.
5. Cook the mixture and add the tomatoes into it.
6. Add the spices.
7. When the tomatoes are done, add the corn into it.
8. Add in the red bell peppers and jalapenos.
9. Mix the ingredients carefully and cover the pan.
10. When the corns are done, add the cilantro and coriander.
11. Mix the ingredients and dish it out in a bowl.

12. Garnish it with avocado slices and sour cream.
13. Your dish is ready to be served.

3.9 Vegetarian Mexican Corn and Potato Casserole Recipe

Preparation Time: 20 minutes
Cooking Time: 20 minutes
Serving: 4

Ingredients:

- Olive oil, two tablespoon
- Eggs, four
- Mozzarella cheese, one cup
- Milk, half cup
- Corn, one cup
- Chopped tomatoes, one cup
- Mexican spice powder, one teaspoon
- Onion, one cup
- Chopped fresh cilantro, as required
- Smoked paprika, half teaspoon
- Hot sauce, half cup
- Potato cubes, one cup

Instructions:
1. Take a pan.

2. Add in the oil and onions.
3. Cook the onions until they become soft and fragrant.
4. Add the tomatoes into the pan.
5. Add the spices.
6. Mix the ingredients carefully and cover your pan.
7. Mix the corn and potato into the mixture.
8. Cook the corn and potatoes.
9. Switch off the stove.
10. When the mixture cools down, add the eggs and milk into it.
11. Pour the casserole mixture in a baking dish.
12. Sprinkle the shredded mozzarella cheese on top.
13. Bake the casserole for twenty minutes.
14. When done, dish it out.
15. Drizzle the hot sauce and sprinkle the cilantro on top.
16. Your dish is ready to be served.

3.10 Vegetarian Mexican Tortilla Soup Recipe

Preparation Time: 30 minutes
Cooking Time: 20 minutes
Serving: 4

Ingredients:

- Olive oil, two tablespoon
- Corn tortillas, four
- Red bell peppers, one cup
- Lime juice, half cup
- Corn, one cup

- Chopped tomatoes, one cup
- Mexican spice powder, one teaspoon
- Onion, one cup
- Chopped fresh cilantro, as required
- Smoked paprika, half teaspoon
- Red pepper paste, half tablespoon
- Black beans, one cup
- Vegetable broth, two cups

Instructions:
1. Take a pan.
2. Add in the oil and onions.
3. Cook the onions until they become soft and fragrant.
4. Add the tomatoes into it.
5. Add the spices.
6. When the tomatoes are done, add the vegetables, corn, beans and stock into it.
7. Add the sliced tortillas and cover the pan.
8. Let the soup cook for ten to fifteen minutes straight.
9. Add cilantro on top.
10. Your dish is ready to be served.

3.11 Mexican Tomatillo Poblano White Beans Recipe

Preparation Time: 10 minutes
Cooking Time: 30 minutes
Serving: 2

Ingredients:

- Minced garlic, two tablespoon

- Red chili pepper, two tablespoon
- Cilantro, half cup
- Chopped coriander, half cup
- Olive oil, two tablespoon
- Chopped tomatoes, one cup
- Dried northern beans, one cup
- Tomatillo sauce, one cup
- Chili powder, one teaspoon
- Red onion, one cup
- Poblano, one cup
- Avocado, one
- Mexican paprika, half teaspoon

Instructions:
1. Take a pan.
2. Add in the oil and red onions.
3. Cook the onions until they become soft and fragrant.
4. Add in the chopped garlic.
5. Cook the mixture and add the tomatoes into it.
6. Add the spices.
7. When the tomatoes are done, add the northern beans into it.
8. Add in the poblano and sauce.
9. Mix the ingredients carefully and cover the pan.
10. When the beans are done, add in the cooked rice, cilantro and coriander.
11. Garnish the dish with chopped avocados.
12. Your dish is ready to be served.

3.12 Vegetarian Mexican Pasta Salad Recipe

Preparation Time: 30 minutes

Cooking Time: 10 minutes
Serving: 4

Ingredients:

- Chiplote sauce, half cup
- Cooked black beans, half cup
- Chopped parsley, half cup
- Chopped green onions, half cup
- Lemon juice, two tablespoon
- Grated cottage cheese, two tablespoon
- Pasta, one cup
- Feta cheese, one cup
- Chopped red cabbage, a quarter cup
- Chopped green cabbage, a quarter cup
- Chopped tomatoes, half cup

Instructions:
1. Take a large bowl.
2. Mix the ingredients together and keep it aside.
3. Boil the pasta according to the package instructions.
4. Drain the pasta.
5. Add the pasta into the bowl.
6. Mix your salad well.
7. Your dish is ready to be served.

3.13 Vegetarian Mexican Taco Casserole Recipe

Preparation Time: 20 minutes
Cooking Time: 20 minutes
Serving: 4

Ingredients:

- Olive oil, two tablespoon
- Eggs, four
- Mozzarella cheese, one cup
- Milk, half cup
- Corn, one cup
- Chopped tomatoes, one cup
- Taco seasoning, two tablespoon
- Onion, one cup
- Bell peppers, one cup
- Chopped fresh cilantro, as required
- Tortilla chips, as required
- Chopped carrots, one cup
- Fresh salsa, half cup
- Avocado cubes, one cup
- Butternut squash, one cup

Instructions:
1. Take a pan.
2. Add in the oil and onions.
3. Cook the onions until they become soft and fragrant.
4. Add the tomatoes into the pan.
5. Add the taco seasoning.
6. Mix the ingredients carefully and cover your pan.
7. Mix the vegetables into the mixture.
8. Cook the vegetables and then switch off the stove.
9. When the vegetables cool, add the eggs and milk into it.
10. Pour the casserole mixture in a baking dish.
11. Sprinkle the shredded mozzarella cheese on top.
12. Bake the casserole for twenty minutes.

13. Add the fresh salsa and avocado cubes on top of the casserole
14. Serve your casserole with tortilla chips.
15. Your dish is ready to be served.

3.14 Vegetarian Mexican Lentil and Cauliflower Rice Tacos Recipe

Preparation Time: 20 minutes
Cooking Time: 20 minutes
Serving: 2

Ingredients:
- Fresh salsa, one cup
- Lentils, one cup
- Tomatoes, two
- Avocado slices, two
- Cilantro, to garnish
- Red onions, one cup
- Taco shells, six
- Mexican chili powder, two teaspoon
- Vegetable oil, one teaspoon
- Salt, to taste
- Pepper, to taste
- Cauliflower rice, one cup
- Hot sauce, half cup
- Cumin powder, one teaspoon

Instructions:
1. Heat a large pan.
2. Add the red onions and vegetable oil into it.
3. Add the chili powder to it.
4. Add the salt and pepper into it.
5. Add the tomatoes into the mixture.

6. Add the hot sauce, lentils and cauliflower rice into the mixture.
7. Cook the mixture for twenty minutes.
8. Heat the taco shells.
9. Once the mixture is cooked add it in the taco shells.
10. Add the fresh salsa on the taco shells.
11. Garnish it with avocado slices and chopped cilantro.
12. Your dish is ready to be served.

3.15 Vegetarian Mexican Quinoa Stuffed Peppers Recipe

Preparation Time: 10 minutes
Cooking Time: 20 minutes
Serving: 2

Ingredients:

- Mexican paprika, half teaspoon
- Water, half cup
- Chili sauce, one cup
- Quinoa, two cups
- Minced garlic, two tablespoon
- Powdered cumin, one tablespoon
- Salt, to taste
- Black pepper, to taste
- Cumin powder, one teaspoon
- Red onion, one cup
- Cilantro, half cup
- Olive oil, two tablespoon
- Bell peppers, four
- Chopped tomatoes, one cup

- Mixed cheese, one cup

Instructions:
1. Take a pan.
2. Add oil and onions into it.
3. Cook the onions until they are fragrant.
4. Add the garlic and mix it until its color changes.
5. Add in the chopped tomatoes.
6. Add the quinoa.
7. Add in the spices, salt, and pepper.
8. Add in the water and cover your pan.
9. Cook the mixture for fifteen minutes.
10. Clean the bell peppers from inside.
11. Add the mixture into the bell peppers.
12. Add the cheese blend on top.
13. Place the bell peppers in a baking tray.
14. Bake the bell peppers for ten minutes.
15. Garnish the cilantro on top.
16. Your dish is ready to be served.

3.16 Vegetarian Mexican Spinach Tortillas Recipe

Preparation Time: 10 minutes
Cooking Time: 20 minutes
Serving: 4

Ingredients:

- Boiling water, three cups
- Unsalted butter, three tablespoon
- Chopped spinach, six cups
- All-purpose flour, three cups
- Kosher salt, half teaspoon

Instructions:
1. Take a large bowl and add the boiling water into the bowl.
2. Add the spinach into the water.
3. Cook the spinach and make sure it is softened.
4. Drain the spinach after two minutes.
5. Add the rest of the ingredients into a food processor.
6. Add the spinach and blend the mixture to form a smooth texture.
7. Add the mixture into a bowl and a little water.
8. Knead the dough.
9. Roll out the dough into tortilla sheets.
10. Cook your spinach tortillas.
11. Serve the tortillas with any dip or sauce you prefer.
12. Your dish is ready to be served.

3.17 Vegetarian Mexican Black Bean Soup Recipe

Preparation Time: 30 minutes
Cooking Time: 20 minutes
Serving: 4

Ingredients:

- Olive oil, two tablespoon
- Black beans, one cup
- Lime juice, half cup
- Chopped tomatoes, one cup
- Mexican spice powder, one teaspoon

- Onion, one cup
- Cumin powder, one teaspoon
- Chopped fresh cilantro, as required
- Smoked paprika, half teaspoon
- Chopped garlic, half tablespoon
- Vegetable broth, two cups

Instructions:
1. Take a pan.
2. Add in the oil and onions.
3. Cook the onions until they become soft and fragrant.
4. Add in the chopped garlic.
5. Cook the mixture and add the tomatoes into it.
6. Add the spices.
7. When the tomatoes are done, add the black beans and rest of the ingredients.
8. Cover the pan.
9. Let the soup cook for ten to fifteen minutes straight.
10. Add cilantro on top.
11. Your dish is ready to be served.

3.18 Vegetarian Mexican Pulled Jackfruit Tacos Recipe

Preparation Time: 20 minutes
Cooking Time: 20 minutes
Serving: 2

Ingredients:

- Fresh salsa, one cup
- Pulled Jackfruit, one cup
- Avocado slices, two
- Cilantro, to garnish
- Red onions, one cup
- Taco shells, six
- Mexican taco sauce, one cup
- Salt, to taste
- Pepper, to taste
- Hot sauce, half cup
- Jalapenos, half cup

Instructions:
1. Heat the taco shells.
2. Mix all the ingredients into the bowl.
3. Add the mixture in the taco shells.
4. Garnish it with avocado slices and chopped cilantro.
5. Your dish is ready to be served.

Chapter 4: The World of Vegetarian Mexican Dessert Recipes

In case you are searching for the absolute best kinds of dessert treats in Mexico, follow these amazing sweet recipes that will make you fall in love with the Mexican deserts forever:

4.1 Vegan Mexican Chocolate Cake Recipe

Preparation Time: 30 minutes
Cooking Time: 10 minutes
Serving: 4

Ingredients:

- All-purpose flour, one cup
- Sugar, one cup
- Mashed bananas, half cup
- Sea salt, as required
- Baking powder, one tablespoon
- Cocoa powder, two tablespoon
- Vegetable oil, half cup
- Low fat milk, half cup
- Egg, two
- Orange juice, for frosting
- Vanilla extract, one teaspoon
- Orange zest, two tablespoon
- Mexican chocolate frosting, as required

Instructions:
1. Add the dried ingredients in a large bowl.
2. Add the low fat milk, vanilla extract, eggs, vegetable oil, orange zest and cocoa powder in a separate bowl.
3. Mix the wet ingredients into the dried ingredients.
4. A semi thick mixture is formed.
5. Add the mashed bananas into the mixture.
6. Add the mixture into a baking tray.
7. Make sure the baking tray is greased properly.
8. Bake the cake for ten to fifteen minutes.
9. Dish out the cake and let it cool down.
10. Brush the orange juice on top of the cake
11. Add the chocolate frosting on top.
12. The dish is ready to be served.

4.2 Vegan Mexican Chocolate Pie Recipe

Preparation Time: 10 minutes
Cooking Time: 30 minutes
Serving: 4

Ingredients:

- Bittersweet chocolate sauce, one cup
- Butter, half cup
- Chocolate shaving, as required
- Pie dough, as required
- Cinnamon powder, a quarter teaspoon
- Vanilla extract, one teaspoon
- Chili powder, a quarter teaspoon
- Silken tofu, one cup
- Butter, for greasing

Instructions:
1. Add the butter in a large bowl and beat it properly.
2. Make it frothy and then add the chocolate sauce.
3. Beat the mixture again and then add the cinnamon powder, vanilla extract and chili powder.
4. Mix the mixture properly.
5. Add the silken tofu and fold the mixture.
6. Lay the pie dough into a greased pie dish.
7. Add the chocolate and tofu mixture on top.
8. Bake the dish properly for ten to fifteen minutes.
9. Add the chocolate shavings on top before serving.
10. The dish is ready to be served.

4.3 Vegan Dessert Nachos with Coffee Ice Cream Recipe

Preparation Time: 10 minutes
Cooking Time: 10 minutes
Serving: 4

Ingredients:

- Whipped coconut cream, two cups
- Cinnamon sugar, half cup
- Rice tortilla chips, one pack
- Chocolate sauce, as required
- Coffee ice cream, two cups
- Chocolate shavings, as required

Instructions:
1. Take a bowl and add the tortilla chips into it.
2. Add the cinnamon sugar on top and place the mixture on a baking tray.
3. Bake the chips for five to ten minutes.
4. Add the coffee ice cream in bowls and add the whipped coconut cream on top of the ice cream.
5. Add the tortilla chips on top.
6. Drizzle the chocolate syrup on the ice cream.
7. Garnish your dish with chocolate shavings.
8. Your dish is ready to be served.

4.4 Vegan Mexican Apple Pie Taquitos Recipe

Preparation Time: 10 minutes
Cooking Time: 30 minutes
Serving: 4

Ingredients:

- Cinnamon spice powder, two tablespoon
- Butter, half cup
- Corn tortillas, four
- Brown sugar, a quarter cup
- Chopped apples, one cup
- Vanilla extract, half teaspoon
- Caramel sauce, one cup
- Coconut oil, two tablespoon

Instructions:
1. Take a large pan.
2. Add the butter and chopped apples into the pan.
3. Add the cinnamon powder, brown sugar and vanilla extract into the pan.
4. Cook the mixture well and then dish it out.

5. Add the formed mixture on top of the tortilla sheets.
6. Roll the mixture and place it in a baking dish.
7. Add the caramel sauce and coconut oil on top.
8. Bake the mixture until it turns golden brown.
9. The dish is ready to be served.

4.5 Vegan Mexican Chocolate and Avocado Mousse Recipe

Preparation time: 30 minutes
Cooking Time: 10 minutes
Serving: 4

Ingredients:

- Mashed avocados, one cup
- Sugar, one cup
- Sea salt, as required
- Baking powder, one tablespoon
- Cocoa powder, two tablespoon
- Low fat milk, half cup
- Egg, two
- Vanilla extract, one teaspoon
- Orange zest, two tablespoon

Instructions:
1. Add the dried ingredients in a large bowl.
2. In a separate bowl, add the low fat milk, vanilla extract, eggs, and cocoa powder.
3. Mix the wet ingredients into the dried ingredients.
4. A semi thick mixture is formed.
5. Cook the formed mixture until it turns thick.
6. Add the avocados into the mixture.

7. Dish out the mousse.
8. The dish is ready to be served.

4.6 Spiced Mexican Chocolate and Coconut Pie Recipe

Preparation Time: 10 minutes
Cooking Time: 30 minutes
Serving: 4

Ingredients:

- Bittersweet chocolate sauce, one cup
- Butter, half cup
- Chocolate shaving, as required
- Pie dough, as required
- Cinnamon powder, a quarter teaspoon
- Vanilla extract, one teaspoon
- Chili powder, a quarter teaspoon
- Coconut cream, one cup
- Shredded coconut shavings, as required
- Butter, for greasing

Instructions:
1. Add the butter in a large bowl and beat it properly.
2. Make it frothy and then add the chocolate sauce.
3. Beat the mixture again and then add the cinnamon powder, vanilla extract and chili powder.
4. Mix the mixture properly.
5. Add the coconut cream and fold the mixture.
6. Lay the pie dough into a greased pie dish.

7. Add the chocolate and coconut cream mixture on top.
8. Bake the dish properly for ten to fifteen minutes.
9. Add the chocolate and coconut shavings on top before serving.
10. The dish is ready to be served.

4.7 Vegan Mexican Churros Recipe

Preparation Time: 10 minutes
Cooking Time: 20 minutes
Serving: 4

Ingredients:

- Water, one cup
- Cinnamon sugar, four teaspoon
- Sugar, one and a half cup
- Baking powder, one teaspoon
- All-purpose flour, two cups
- Vegetable oil, as required

Instructions:
1. Add the all-purpose flour in a large bowl.
2. Add the sugar into the bowl.
3. Add the baking powder into the bowl and mix it.
4. Add the water into it.
5. Form a semi-thick mixture.
6. Pour the mixture into a pipping bag.
7. Heat the vegetable oil in a large pan.
8. Add a little mixture one by one through the pipping bag into the oil.

9. Cook the churros until they turn golden brown.
10. Add the cinnamon sugar on top.
11. Your dish is ready to be served.

4.8 Vegan Mexican Conchas Recipe

Preparation Time: 10 minutes
Cooking Time: 20 minutes
Serving: 4

Ingredients:

- Soy milk, one cup
- Bread flour, two cup
- Active dry yeast, two teaspoon
- Granulated sugar, one cup
- Mashed sweet potatoes, half cup
- Butter, half cup
- Salt, to taste

For topping:
- Cinnamon sugar, as required

Instructions:
1. Take a large bowl.
2. Add all the ingredients into the bowl.
3. Mix to form a dough structure.
4. Use the concha cutter to cut the dough into conchas.
5. Place the conchas on a baking tray.
6. Bake the conchas.
7. Add the cinnamon sugar on top.
8. Your dish is ready to be served.

4.9 Vegan Champurrado Recipe

Preparation Time: 10 minutes
Cooking Time: 40 minutes
Serving: 4

Ingredients:

- Corn flour, a quarter cup
- Dark brown sugar, one cup
- Cocoa powder, one tablespoon
- Cayenne pepper, half teaspoon
- Kosher salt, half teaspoon
- Almond milk, one cup
- Vanilla extract, one teaspoon
- Whipped cream, as required
- Water, two cups
- Bittersweet chocolate, half cup

Instructions:
1. Take a large sauce pan.
2. Add the water into the pan and heat it.
3. When the water almost reaches the boiling temperature add the rest of the ingredients except the milk, whipped cream and chocolate into the pan.
4. Cook the mixture for ten minutes approximately.
5. Add the almond milk and chocolate into the mixture.
6. Cook the mixture for five minutes.
7. Pour the mixture into cups.
8. Garnish the dish with the whipped cream on top.
9. Your dish is ready to be served.

4.10 Vegan Mexican Flan Recipe

Preparation Time: 10 minutes
Cooking Time: 20 minutes
Serving: 4

> **Ingredients:**
>
> - Corn flour, one cup
> - Baking powder, four teaspoon
> - Baking soda, one teaspoon
> - Buttermilk, two cups
> - White sugar, one cup
> - Water, two cups
> - Tapioca flour, one cup
> - Coconut cream, half cup
> - Caramel, one cup

Instructions:
1. Add the tapioca flour in a large bowl.
2. Add the corn flour into the mixture.
3. Add the white sugar and beat the mixture for five more minutes.
4. Add all the dried ingredients in a separate bowl.
5. Add the water into it.
6. Add the coconut cream into the mixture.
7. Cook the mixture in a saucepan thoroughly until a homogeneous mixture is obtained.
8. Add the caramel in a dish and pour the flan mixture.
9. Let the flan cool down and then flip it on a dish upside down.

10. Your dish is ready to be served.

4.11 Vegan Mexican Spiced Chocolate and Avocado Pudding Recipe

Preparation Time: 30 minutes
Cooking Time: 10 minutes
Serving: 4

Ingredients:

- Cinnamon powder, one teaspoon
- Mashed avocados, one cup
- Sugar, one cup
- Sea salt, as required
- Baking powder, one tablespoon
- Cocoa powder, two tablespoon
- Low fat milk, half cup
- Egg, two
- Cayenne pepper, one teaspoon
- Nutmeg, one teaspoon
- Vanilla extract, one teaspoon
- Corn flour, two tablespoon

Instructions:
1. Add the dried ingredients in a large bowl.
2. Add the low fat milk, vanilla extract, cinnamon powder, eggs, nutmeg, cayenne pepper and cocoa powder in a separate bowl.
3. Mix the wet ingredients into the dried ingredients.
4. A semi thick mixture is formed.
5. Cook the formed mixture until it turns thick.
6. Add the avocados into the mixture.
7. Dish out the pudding.

8. The dish is ready to be served.

4.12 Mexican Chocolate Doughnuts Recipe

Preparation Time: 50 minutes
Cooking Time: 40 minutes
Serving: 2

Ingredients:

- Eggs, two
- Yeast, half cup
- Cocoa powder, one tablespoon
- Maple syrup, one tablespoon
- Coconut milk, half cup
- White sugar, half cup
- Salt, one teaspoon
- Vanilla extract, one tablespoon
- Cake flour, two cups
- Butter, one cup
- Chocolate syrup

Instructions:
1. Take a medium bowl and add the eggs, cocoa powder and the cake flour in it.
2. Add one cup coconut milk and mix well.
3. Add the sugar, salt and the beaten eggs.
4. Mix them well.
5. Mix the warm milk mixture with the flour and the coconut.
6. Add the eggs and vanilla extract together.
7. Add the yeast into the whole mixture.

8. When dough is formed, roll it in your desired shape.
9. Place the doughnuts on a greased baking tray.
10. Bake the doughnuts for twenty minutes.
11. Garnish the doughnuts with chocolate syrup.
12. Your dish is ready to be served.

4.13 Mexican Carlota de Limon Recipe

Preparation Time: 10 minutes
Cooking Time: 30 minutes
Serving: 4

Ingredients:

- Bittersweet chocolate sauce, one cup
- Butter, half cup
- Chocolate shaving, as required
- Lemon juice, half cup
- Cinnamon powder, a quarter teaspoon
- Vanilla extract, one teaspoon
- Chili powder, a quarter teaspoon
- Butter, for greasing

Instructions:
1. Add the butter in a large bowl and beat it properly.
2. Make it frothy and then add the chocolate sauce.
3. Beat the mixture again and then add the cinnamon powder, vanilla extract and chili powder.
4. Mix the mixture properly.
5. Add the lemon juice and fold the mixture.

6. Lay the crushed biscuits in a dish.
7. Add a little chocolate and lemon mixture on top.
8. Add another layer of the crushed biscuits and repeat the procedure.
9. Add the chocolate shavings on top before serving.
10. The dish is ready to be served.

4.14 Mexican Hot Chocolate Recipe

Preparation Time: 10 minutes
Cooking Time: 40 minutes
Serving: 4

Ingredients:

- Dark brown sugar, one cup
- Cocoa powder, one tablespoon
- Cayenne pepper, half teaspoon
- Kosher salt, half teaspoon
- Almond milk, one cup
- Chili powder, one teaspoon
- Whipped cream, as required
- Water, two cups

Instructions:
1. Take a large sauce pan.
2. Add the water into the pan and heat it.
3. When the water almost reaches the boiling temperature, add the rest of the ingredients except the milk, and whipped cream into the pan.
4. Cook the mixture for ten minutes approximately.
5. Add the almond milk into the mixture.
6. Cook the mixture for five minutes.
7. Pour the mixture into cups.
8. Garnish the dish with the whipped cream on top.

9. Your dish is ready to be served.

4.15 Vegan Mexican Margarita Fruit Coupe Recipe

Preparation Time: 10 minutes
Cooking Time: 5 minutes
Serving: 2

Ingredients:

- Persimmon, two
- Mango cubes, one cup
- Granulated sugar, one tablespoon
- Maple syrup, one tablespoon
- Orange juice, half cup
- Salt, half teaspoon
- Kiwi, one cup
- Mint leaves, as required
- Lime juice, one tablespoon
- Tequilla, two cups

Instructions:
1. Add all the ingredients into a bowl.
2. Mix well and add it into small bowls.
3. Garnish the coupe with fresh mint leaves.
4. Your dish is ready to be served.

Chapter 5: The World of Vegetarian Mexican Snack Recipes

Snacks originated from Mexico are famous throughout the world. Following are some amazing snack recipes that are rich in healthy nutrients and you can easily make them with the detailed instructions list in each recipe:

5.1 Mexican Carrot Fries Recipe

Preparation Time: 10 minutes
Cooking Time: 15 minutes
Serving: 4

Ingredients:

- Avocado, one
- Eggs, two
- Cold water, two tablespoon
- Carrots, three
- Salt, half tablespoon
- Pepper, half tablespoon
- Fresh salsa, two tablespoon
- Red chili, one
- Coriander leaves, three to four
- Red onion, one
- Oil, one cup

Instructions:
1. Take a large bowl and add the eggs in it
2. Add the cold water in it and mix well.
3. Add the salt and pepper into it.

4. Mix well until a good mixture is obtained.
5. Add the carrot slices and coat them with the egg mixture.
6. Then add the red onion into it.
7. Add the red chili and little oil to have a consistent mixture.
8. Heat the oil in a saucepan.
9. Fry the carrots in it until they are light brown.
10. Your dish is ready to be served.

5.2 Black Bean and Corn Salsa Recipe

Preparation Time: 10 minutes
Cooking Time: 10 minutes
Serving: 2

Ingredients:

- Whole kernel corn, one can
- Black beans, one cup
- Chopped red onions, half cup
- Olive oil, one tablespoon
- Salt, half teaspoon
- Cilantro, one tablespoon
- Fresh lime juice, two tablespoon
- Chile pepper, one teaspoon

Instructions:
1. Add the black beans in a large bowl.
2. Add the whole kernel corns into it.
3. Add the red onions in the bowl.
4. Mix all the ingredients well.
5. Add the lime juice into it.

6. Add the salt and pepper in it.
7. Add little oil to get a consistent mixture.
8. Refrigerate it for thirty minutes.
9. Your dish is ready to be served.

5.3 Traditional Mexican Vegetarian Chilaquiles Rojos Recipe

Preparation Time: 10 minutes
Cooking Time: 40 minutes
Serving: 4

Ingredients:

- Corn tortillas, ten
- Jalapeno, one
- White onion, half
- Peeled garlic, two
- Cumin, half teaspoon
- Salt, half teaspoon
- Chicken broth, one cup
- Vegetable oil, one tablespoon
- Whole tomatoes, one can
- Eggs, two
- Beans, half cup
- Avocado, as required
- Mexican crema, as needed
- Radish slices, two

Instructions:
1. Bake the tortillas for fifteen minutes.
2. Place the tomatoes, jalapeno, onions, garlic, vegetable oil in a large bowl.

3. Add the salt and cumin as needed.
4. Blend the all ingredients to have a consistent mixture.
5. Then cook this mixture for ten minutes.
6. Add the chicken broth in cooking mixture.
7. Transfer the baked chips to the skillet.
8. Fold it gently into the sauce.
9. Simmer it for five minutes.
10. Your dish is ready to be served.

5.4 Vegetarian Mexican Empanadas Recipe

Preparation Time: 30 minutes
Cooking Time: 10 minutes
Serving: 4

Ingredients:

- Butter milk biscuits, eight
- Black beans, one can
- Tomato sauce, three tablespoon
- Dried oregano, half teaspoon
- Garlic powder, one teaspoon
- Milk, as needed
- Salsa, as needed
- Oil, one tablespoon
- Little cilantro
- Chili powder, half teaspoon

Instructions:
1. Wash the beans with water thoroughly.
2. Mash the beans with a potato masher.
3. Add the oil in the skillet.

4. Add the mashed beans, crushed tomatoes, chili powder and garlic powder in it.
5. Add the oregano in the same skillet.
6. Fry all the ingredients for two minutes until the ingredients combine well.
7. Transfer it to the bowl and let it cool.
8. Add the cilantro as needed.
9. Take the biscuits and roll them in your desired shape.
10. Then place the filling in each of biscuits.
11. Sprinkle the milk over it.
12. Place the empanadas over the baking sheet.
13. Bake it for ten minutes until it becomes golden brown.
14. Then you can add salt if required.
15. Your dish is ready to be served.

5.5 Vegetarian Mexican Tortilla with Tangy Guacamole Recipe

Preparation Time: 30 minutes
Cooking Time: 50 minutes
Serving: 4

Ingredients:

- Corn tortillas, five
- White onion, half
- Peeled garlic, two
- Cumin, half teaspoon
- Salt, half teaspoon
- Vegetable oil, one tablespoon
- Whole tomatoes, one can
- Eggs, two

- Beans, half cup
- Avocado, as required

Instructions:
1. Take a large bowl and add white onions.
2. Add the ginger and garlic powder.
3. Mix well until a good mixture is obtained.
4. Add the cumin and salt into it and mix gently.
5. The guacamole is ready to use.
6. Place the tortillas on a baking tray and bake them for ten minutes.
7. Serve the tortillas with the already prepared guacamole.

5.6 Vegetarian Mexican Cauliflower Tacos Recipe

Preparation Time: 20 minutes
Cooking Time: 20 minutes
Serving: 2

Ingredients:

- Fresh salsa, one cup
- Tomatoes, two
- Avocado slices, two
- Cilantro, to garnish
- Red onions, one cup
- Taco shells, six
- Mexican chili powder, two teaspoon
- Vegetable oil, one teaspoon
- Salt, to taste
- Pepper, to taste
- Chopped cauliflower florets, one cup

- Hot sauce, half cup
- Cumin powder, one teaspoon

Instructions:
1. Heat a large pan.
2. Add the red onions and vegetable oil into it.
3. Add the chili powder to it.
4. Add the salt and pepper into it.
5. Add the tomatoes into the mixture.
6. Add the hot sauce, and the cauliflower florets into the mixture.
7. Cook the mixture for twenty minutes.
8. Heat the taco shells.
9. Once the mixture is cooked, add it in the taco shells.
10. Add the fresh salsa on the taco shells.
11. Garnish it with avocado slices and chopped cilantro.
12. Your dish is ready to be served.

5.7 Mexican Apricot and Avocado Salad Recipe

Preparation Time: 30 minutes
Cooking Time: 10 minutes
Serving: 4

Ingredients:

- Onions, one
- Chopped garlic, one teaspoon
- Mexican hot sauce, half cup
- Chopped cilantro, half tablespoon
- Apricot cubes, two cups
- Tortilla chips, as required
- Fresh salsa, half cup
- Avocado slices, one cup
- Salt, to taste
- Black pepper, to taste
- Chopped fresh chives, as required
- Mexican salad dressing, one cup

Instructions:
1. Take a large bowl.
2. Add all the ingredients into the bowl.
3. Mix all the ingredients well.
4. Add the tortilla chips on top of the salad.
5. Your dish is ready to be served.

5.8 Mexican Sweet Potato Nachos Recipe

Preparation Time: 10 minutes
Cooking Time: 15 minutes
Serving: 4

Ingredients:

- Cold water, half cup
- Sweet potatoes, three
- Salt, half tablespoon

- Pepper, half tablespoon
- Red chili, one
- Coriander leaves, three to four
- Oil, one cup

Instructions:
1. Take a large bowl
2. Add the cold water and sweet potato slices in it and mix well.
3. Add the salt and pepper into another bowl.
4. Add the red chili also in the bowl.
5. Mix well until a good mixture is obtained.
6. Add the sweet potato slices in the bowl.
7. Add the oil in the mixture.
8. Bake the sweet potato slices in it until light brown color comes.
9. Your dish is ready to be served.

5.9 Mexican Tofu Tacos with Chili Lime Slaw Recipe

Preparation Time: 20 minutes
Cooking Time: 20 minutes
Serving: 2

Ingredients:

- Chili lime slaw, one cup
- Chopped tofu, one cup
- Tomatoes, two
- Avocado slices, two
- Cilantro, to garnish
- Red onions, one cup
- Taco shells, six
- Mexican chili powder, two teaspoon
- Vegetable oil, one teaspoon
- Salt, to taste
- Pepper, to taste
- Hot sauce, half cup
- Cumin powder, one teaspoon

Instructions:
1. Heat a large pan.
2. Add the red onions and vegetable oil into it.
3. Add the chili powder to it.
4. Add the salt and pepper into it.
5. Add the tomatoes into the mixture.
6. Add the hot sauce, and the chopped tofu into the mixture.
7. Cook the mixture for twenty minutes.
8. Heat the taco shells.
9. Once the mixture is cooked, add it in the taco shells.
10. Add the chili lime slaw on the taco shells.
11. Garnish it with avocado slices and chopped cilantro.
12. Your dish is ready to be served.

5.10 Mexican Potato Skins Recipe

Preparation Time: 10 minutes

Cooking Time: 15 minutes
Serving: 4
Ingredients:

- Cold water, half cup
- Potato peels, three
- Salt, half tablespoon
- Pepper, half tablespoon
- Red chili, one
- Coriander leaves, three to four
- Oil, one cup

Instructions:
1. Take a large bowl.
2. Add the cold water and potato peels in it and mix well.
3. Drain the water and dry the potato peels.
4. Add the salt and pepper into it another bowl.
5. Add the potato peels in the bowl.
6. Add the oil and chili in the mixture.
7. Bake the potato peels in it until light brown color comes.
8. Your dish is ready to be served.

Conclusion

Mexican cooking is a significant part of the lifestyle, social design and mainstream customs of Mexico. The main illustration of this association is the utilization of traditional food in events and occasions, especially in the South and Central locales of the country.

Mexican cooking is unbelievably vast and astonishing. It began from Mexico yet has spread worldwide and it is eventually revered and eaten at so many places in the world. The people of the United States of America love Mexican food and they eat it reliably.

This book covers the life of a Mexican who eats only vegetarian food, making it easy for them to prepare their favourite recipes inside their kitchen without any stress. This cookbook incorporates 70 healthy recipes that contain vegetarian breakfast recipes, vegetarian lunch and dinner recipes, vegetarian snack recipes and vegetarian dessert recipes that have Mexican origin and taste. So, start cooking today with this amazing and easy cookbook.

Printed in Great Britain
by Amazon